The Dao of
Math and Science

Ireality El

The Dao of
Math and Science

A Manual For the Student
of Life/Light
by Ireality El

This book is dedicated to my children, Rakhem and Isis, to Man, Wombman, and Child; Sun, Moon, and Stars, the entire Human Family of Earth-land, and, in memory of Salvatore Arcuri

Special mention to Professor I Self, Vishnu Allah-Din Shabazz, C.M. Bey, Noble Drew Ali, Clarence 13 The Father, Thoth The Atlantean, Confucius, Lao Tzu, Buddha, Jesus, Mohammed, and all the Prophets who have walked and walk this Earth as even some go unrecognized.

Contents

Introduction

I have known Ireality for many creations and am honored to write this introduction for such a great comrade and warrior. I have watched him elevate and, at times, have aided him in his development.

Ireality is a student of the Universal Divine Principles that have always existed, these principles are the basis for all "creation" both cosmically and earthbound. Ireality has a skilled background in research and the ability to show and prove in a matter of minutes.

It is with a pure heart that I met this brother back in the early nineties when he was finding his way. Since then, I have witnessed Ireality move into the sciences of Chi Kung, numerology, cosmogony, sacred geometry, Al Kemi, Buddhism, Islaam, etc.

The studies are endless as they should be and Ireality

is a "student" who has become a "teacher." As I am also still a student and it is this type of humility that I find with my comrade Ireality. He is one of the most peaceful souls I know but even peace can be disturbed and Irealz's peace you do not want to disturb because the outcome would not be healthy.

Ireality has a way with his words, he is profound yet simple and anyone can understand his writings and his wisdom. Ireality is a father who loves his seeds immensely as I have witnessed their interactions. He is a great soul with much to offer and anyone can learn from my brother and my comrade.

This book is straight fire and I hope that many will gain from the perspective, wisdom and insight of Ireality El's "kitaab" (book). This book is an asset to anyone who is seeking "balance" because this is the "Tao" (the way) to become enlightened and to align with Universal principles and ancient wisdom. I hope you all enjoy as I have.

HONORS to my Comrade, I stand with you, brother, at all times.

Peace,

Prof. I Self

Age of Aquarius!

"All teachings are mere references. The true experience is living your own life. Then, even the holiest of words are only words."

"Those who don't know how to suffer are the worst off. There are times when the only correct thing we can do is to bear out troubles until a better day."

Deng Ming-Dao

Spiritual War

◇◇◇◇◇◇

There are ways but the Way is uncharted; There are names but not nature in words: Nameless indeed is the source of creation.

Something there is, whose veiled creation was. Before the earth or sky began to be; So silent, so aloof and so alone, It Changes not, nor fails, but touches all: Conceive it as the mother of All. I do not know its name: A name for it is Way/Dao. I Call it Great.

Dao De Ching

Let it be known that I, Ireality El aka Christoth Maat Arcuri El, do not claim to be the founder of the Supreme Math and Science Applied to Life/Light; as there is nothing new under the Sun. This is merely a culmination of the lessons and studies I have knowledged and experienced on my path to enlightenment. This is my Innerstanding and contribution to Humanity. I will combine Numerology, which is Supreme

Mathematics Scale 0-9, along with the science of Astrology and Magnetics as it can be applied to day to day life in a universal manner for all people. We will deal with Math and Science of Life/Light in order to better innerstand ourselves, our families and friends, and to establish a system of morals and values according to nature so that we may uplift our own communities and all of fallen humanity.

This will be done in the most universal way, as it is time for all of the human families to unite for the common good and our great planet Earth. All is one and one is all. So violating one, in turn, violates yourself and all. We are only as strong as our weakest link and that is why it is up to us to uplift our fellow brothers and sistars that comprise the whole human family.

We are spiritual beings and there is no superior race. There are at least seven shades of melanin through the great process of amalgamation that has taken place since ancient times. Those who cannot evolve to learn to love, live, and grow with all humanity as one will surely devolve. Life is a blessing and equal are all races/nationalities, shades, and creeds according to nature. In all actuality, race is an idea. When you play the "Race Game" you automatically lose. If there were truly different races amongst the human family we would not be able to interbreed.

When you are content to simply be yourself, and do not compare or compete, everyone will respect you. Dao De Ching, 8.

It is great to pay homage to the great ancient civilizations of the planet who achieved higher levels than that of today and to learn as much as possible from their lives and cultures.

Humanity cannot and will not survive a physical war. But, can humanity survive a spiritual war? Yes, indeed!

Those who are bound by desire only see the outward container. Dao De Ching

This will serve as a reference guide to focus on the positive energies of the day through the language of Mathematics and Science. Since ancient times, languages had numerical and mathematic values and incorporated the visual power of symbols. We will review and break down certain signs and symbols as they are working tools of the mind which help us navigate the physical world. We will deal in Math and Science because these are actual facts.

No offense to anyone but religion as taught by certain clergymen, tends to cause confusion and division amongst our human family; to the point of war. This is not attacking religion for it is not religion's fault. Instead, it is the fault of those clergy who teach in a biased manner which is not equality. Actually, religion in its nature is spirituality and represents the Divine Laws of Man/Wombman/Child. It is those that strive to control the masses and the world's resources that love to cause confusion and division amongst the human family and, at times, they use religion as a tool to do so.

I am for Divine Religion which is Spiritual Cultivation of the mind, body, and soul in order to raise one's vibration or frequency so one may become more in tune and one with the Universal Source/Creation/God/Allah/etc. This is the purpose of all religion. Religion also stems from the Sun, Moon, and Stars; the Universal Flag that flies true over all our heads. From ancient times, this Universal Flag has been honored as it guides civilization starting with the basic root of Agriculture and Navigation. You see, one must be in tune with Astrology and follow the cycles to be a good farmer and grow food. This is civilization and civilization = self sufficiency.

In my honest opinion, Buddhism and Taoism/Daoism are Supreme in nature because they focus on being one with, and living according to, nature. There is only one universal truth and it is expressed in different ways throughout all of the religions. Christianity, Judaism, Islam, etc., whose Prophets came to a people at a certain period of time, speaking the language of the people so that they could better understand the message.

In fact, the Prophet Jesus and the Prophet Mohammed (peace be upon them) were both descendents of the Biblical Abraham. This makes them distant cousins related through their bloodlines. Also, some 1500-2000 years before Jesus or Mohammed in Khemit (Egypt is the Greek name), Ahkenaton taught monotheism; the belief in one "God." This "God" represented both Feminine and Masculine principles.

Many Khemitic words are present in the Arabic language including Allah and Kabba. From the Kabba comes the Kabballah, originally an ancient Khemitian system of divination and cultivation, adopted by Judaism.

We give the utmost respect and recognition to all Prophets. Thirty-six thousand years ago there was Thoth who gave the Emerald Tablets, Confucius to Buddha to Lao Tzu and lineage from Jesus to Mohammad, peace be upon all of them.

Chinese civilization along the yellow river is recorded some 5,000 years ago. The elders claim 7,000/9,000 years, however, they humbly give credit to a "prehistoric" civilization that enlightened them. They practiced Spiritual Cultivation through meditation and postures. This would be referred to as religion but the term religion was not coined yet. If you look at prayer postures you will see that they derived from meditation postures, such as Qigong and Yoga, which by historical records predate what is known today as religion.

Based on my studies, the oldest scripture is The Emerald Tablets, written by Thoth, The Atlantean, some 36,000 years ago. Thoth is also known as Tahuti, Enoch, Hermes, and Chiram, the sone of a widow. The Emeral Tablets go back to the days of Atlantis and Mu/Lemuria. I have a translated copy and it is very specific on spiritual practices and even includes what to do upon dying and exiting the human temple/body. The scripture also translates the process of astral travel. I am now sharing my experiences through study and Cultivation Practice.

At a certain point of overstanding, Man/Wombman becomes that which he/she knows. The Prophets were the Word in the Flesh. They were the living example. They were the point of reference for all humanity. Divine Love is the only healing force for the entire human family. If one suffers, we all suffer. It is time for all to be healed.

What the wise man seeks is within himself, what the fool seeks is within others. Analects of Confucius 15:20

You see, nowadays, most people need all types of scientific studies to prove to them what is "real." In all actuality, these scientists are discovering nothing new, only re-affirming that which was already known. So how did the Prophets, Daoist and Buddhist Priests know these ultimate truths? They knew through looking inward through Spiritual Cultivation Practices and simply by observing nature, the Sun, Moon, and Stars, and the rhythmic patterns recorded therein. They walked, talked, lived and breathed that which they knew to be true. They observed the divine. They were able to see the connectedness of all life. They were that which they know. And yes, it is that simple, and yes, what a blessing. So now, again we can become responsible and start to look inward as well. And that is the great lesson.

Now, let us look further. Those in tune do not need these scientific studies to prove certain obvious truths of nature and life. For example, a scientist could do a study on the Pineal Gland and explain how the 3rd Eye opens and one could read the study and say, "Yes, this is true based on this study." However, one really doesn't know this unless one sits in meditation and experiences the opening of the 3rd Eye/Pineal Gland.

Indeed the Wise Man's office is to work by being still. Dao De

Ching on Meditation

The Chinese have preserved, mastered, and passed down the Spiritual Cultivation Practices of Qigong (Chi Gong) for at least 5,000 years. Qi/Chi translates as the life-force energy that exists within us all and throughout the Universe. Gong translates as work or accomplishment of effort. So, Qigong translates as the cultivation of one's life-force. This is done through postures and breathing methods where one circulates the life-force essence/DNA making the flesh into Flesh Divine. This is done through the Holy Breath. The Breath is Life. (As this is not a book on Qigong, my next book will be dedicated to Qigong and will further elaborate). However, the Elders of the Taoist/Daoist Cultivation Systems and The Buddha Fa School Systems state that this was passed down from a "pre-historic" civilization.

The point here is that Qigong, Yoga, etc., also known as the Spiritual Cultivation Practices/meditations, were in fact the foundation of religions. All religious texts are merely allegorical stories of spiritual alchemy/cultivation practices, also known as prayer/meditations, in addition to the sciences of Astrology and Cosmology. All religious prayer postures, from Christianity to Judaism to Islam, are derived from Spiritual Cultivation postures. Yoga is another cultivation system that was developed from the battle between Buddhism and Brahamism which turned into Hinduism. The Spiritual Cultivation Practices/ meditations focus on looking and turning inward for all the answers one needs. You become one with self, nature, and the universe. We must be that which we are...divine. Sitting still in meditation and quieting the mind is a skill.

This is nothing new but instead it is ancient science. In India, there is an ancient Iron Pillar that is 99.9% iron and modern day smelting technologies cannot duplicate this. The pyramids are another example. The Greeks named them pyramids while the original name is Muurs.

All Muurs are aligned with constellations and one of their uses could have been for teleporting to other planets or astral travel. The Muurs also used the power of aligning crystals which served as great generators of power. The Great Obelisks served as connectors to this great energy all over the earth. You see, these Muurs were constructed on all continents according to the energy grid of the planet. In other words, they were built very strategically to align with the energy grid of the planet so that they could serve as great generators of power.

Crystals are great energy conductors whose magnetic fields emit various kinds of energy. Crystals can be used to balance energies in the body and aura, to cleanse the energy centers of the body, or, on a much greater level, like the ancients who used them with the Muurs/pyramids and obelisks to light up and give power to this planet. The science of the pi equation and the true science of man dwell within the Muurs.

Additionally, there are great chambers that dwell under the Earth in which you can find magnificent crystals of every kind. Why? I will leave you with questions in order to spark thought☺.

In 1609, they say Galileo invented the telescope, however, in the National Museum in the University of Peru there is a rock carving that depicts a man looking through a telescope which carbon dates to at least 27,000 years ago. There is nothing new under the Sun. Is man-made technology really advanced?

We are all glandular beings so let's look at the pineal

gland which is referred to as the 3rd Eye. The pineal gland is located between and behind the two physical eyes.

The physical eyes block us from being able to see beyond this dimension with our 3rd Eye/Pineal Gland. However, when the 3rd Eye is fully opened, it is able to move at 24 frames per second and in full color. This is the science of films. The television and other man made technologies are inhibiting us from our natural abilities.

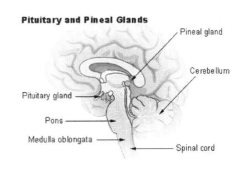

Pituitary and Pineal Glands

Pineal gland

Cerebellum

Pituitary gland

Pons

Medulla oblongata

Spinal cord

We still possess supernatural abilities that we can tune into but, we can only access them thru Spiritual Practices and good Moral Character. Good Moral Character is pure heart and mind intention. This is known as XinXing (shinshing). The universe will not allow you to have these abilities if you have poor or bad moral character. The Universe understands intention and simple selfish acts close and clogs the pineal gland. The pineal gland and the pituitary gland work together, hand in hand. The pituitary gland serves as messenger to the pineal gland. It is said that you will find Heaven in the Land of Milk and Honey. Well, the pineal gland secretes a whitish, milky substance called melatonin and the pituitary gland secretes a golden, honey-like substance. The Pituitary Gland also secretes many other hormones, such as, the Human Growth Hormone or HGH. Again, Heaven is in the Mind☺.

Be Still while you work. And keep full control of All. Dao De Ching

Please bear in mind that anyone who has hate as a part of their doctrine is a False Prophet and is causing separation and confusion amongst the masses. Universal Divine Love is the only cure for the entire Human Family. We can only win a Spiritual War and this is a war that starts within self. Noble Drew Ali taught of "a war that cannot be told in words." Instead, here we look deeper at the war within self; the war between the higher self (the mind) and the lower self (the body).

The higher self represents what is right and exact; the higher conscious mind. The lower self represents the body, the carnal fleshly desires that can easily distract us, murky ethers, such as, materialism aka greed, lust, gluttony, racism, cheating, over-sexing, coveting another's spouse, murder, etc.

Herein we see the principles of exercising Mind/The Higher Self over Matter/The Lower Self. We also learn the principles of what is right and what is wrong universally and how we should be responsible for our own actions. This also represents the supreme balance of positive and negative which is also translated as good and evil. This is the true war that cannot be told in words. This is the war that all humanity must win within self before we can ever achieve peace and harmony amongst the entire human family.

You see fear is one of the biggest factors in dealing with the lower self. It is out of fear that one wants to be in control of another. It is out of fear that one wants to rule the world. It is an inner fear or insecurity that makes man jealous or envious thus creating the momentum for hate, materialism for wrong reasons, etc. It is this insecurity that would drive one to commit sins against others and upon oneself.

So this is why we must build up the confidence of the higher self. This must be done by exercising ones will and mind intention. One can only achieve this through hard work and discipline. Discipline of the mind, body, and soul.

A religion warring against another is a total contradiction and a reflection of wrong teachings.

The Wise man teaches not by speech, but by accomplishment; He does for everything/everyone, neglecting none. Dao De Ching

The Time is Now

◇◇◇◇◇◇

The Way is a void, Used but never filled: An abyss it is, Like an ancestor from which all things come.

A deep pool it is, Never to run dry! Whose offspring it may be I do not know: It is like a preface to God.

The Sky is everlasting And the Earth is very old. Why so? Because the world exists not for itself; it can and will live on.

The wise man chooses to be last. And by doing so he becomes first of all. Dao De Ching

The Earth has had many names and has a history of at least 4.5 billion years. So those that claim to know the whole history of the Earth and claim a certain status are certainly on the wrong path. Man/woman does not and cannot truly own anything on this earth plane and those in search of dominance and ownership over its so-called dominion and people surely cause destruction, chaos, and confusion. This earth has exploded and the magnetic poles have shifted at least nine times already and probably more. The Sumerians spoke of this planet once being connected to a twin planet called Nibiru. They taught of a time when the poles shifted causing Nibiru to be spit out of the Earth/Terra and that Nibiru traveled to the Sirius Constellation where it remained in cipher. This also means that life exists on Nibiru. Would we be so arrogant to think that we are the only intelligent life forms that exist throughout the cosmos?

Astronomers know of Nibiru's existence but they cannot see it with their telescopic technology. They call it the "Dark Planet" and know it exists because of the extreme vibrational influence it has been having on Neptune and Uranus knocking them out of their regular orbits. When the Earth's magnetic poles shift we will come back into contact with Nibiru.

They have been also speaking of a Supernova which they call "Betelguese" and that when it exploded it had the potential to become a black hole or a new Sun. I say exploded because as I write this, it just exploded and from China to Africa. The aftermath was seen as a Dual Sun image which was photographed and video recorded on March 5, 2011. Some scientists have dismissed it as a mirage or abnormal refraction while other scientists say that it does not fit the description of a

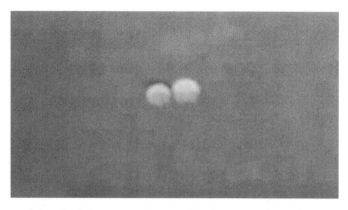

mirage. If it had been a mirage, the focus and position would change in relation to the camera's moves and this was not the case. Is this Nibiru returning? Will we reunite with our Brothers and Sistars from Nibiru? Or, maybe not? Maybe two planets in the same cipher/galaxy that exhibit life that flourishes cannot dwell in the same galaxy? Maybe it will be destruction? Or, a new beginning? Or, maybe it is possible? Who knows? You see the questions are great, great to spark the mind and expand the possibilities. However does one truly know? When one becomes one with the All, the All is possible. The universe is infinite and forever expanding and the realms are far too much for most human minds to handle or even imagine. So, we must realize that this is ok.

And so this is the point, the mind's eye, the imagination. These thoughts of inspiration and imagination spark growth and stimulation to the mind opening new channels and pathways in the mind forever expanding as the universe does. In this way we can tap into the infinite. One never truly forgets anything, all of one's experiences via the senses are recorded into your brainwaves and this forms creases.

We must simply observe the cycles of nature, reflect, and do the knowledge to the patterns. This is to gain wisdom and to gain understanding of life as it occurs naturally around us. And it is ok to keep it that simple. It is ok to get more complex and scientific in an effort to explain these magnificent laws of creation. However, when man creates technology which goes against and harms nature, this is when we know and can show and prove how and why it is wrong. Overstand?

Every 26,000 years the Earth renews its history. This happens when the Earth travels backward through all of the Zodiac Constellations in our Galaxy. This is the poles shifting north to south and south to north. We are in the cosmic womb of the universe. If you look at a child in the womb, what happens right before the birth? The child flips inside the womb with the head shifting to where the feet were and vice versa.

Right now the poles have already been shifting forty miles each year toward Russia. This reflects a change in the Earth's core (which is actually another Sun; yes we have two

Suns). This process is being sped up due to oil corporations and governments constantly stealing the Earth's Black Blood aka Oil which is forbidden. They even had to shut down the Tampa Florida International Airport for one week to renumber the north-south runway to reflect its new magnetic alignment. Look at the Earthquake in Japan at the end of January 2011 that shook the Earth. According to modern scientists, this was the biggest Earthquake "history" has known. This is the result of the poles and the tectonic plates shifting. There will be only more disasters, earthquakes, tornados, floods, etc., to come. I suggest if you live near any coastal area, you move at least five hundred miles inland.

In 2011, on the winter solstice, there was a lunar eclipse followed by a solar eclipse twenty days later. Anytime this happens, there will be major changes on the Earth. An event like this has not happened in at least a millennium and will result in changes in the weather, atmosphere, species, and vibrational frequency of the planet. In the next two to three years we will move from orgon vibration to a more magnetic vibration. When this happens, the vibration will knock out the satellites and electricity as they will not be able to exist. We must raise our vibrations as much as possible to survive these changes or we will devolve instead of evolve. We may very well enter into a more ethereal plane where we see beyond the illusion of this material plane and see true reality. Those who have not raised their vibration will not be able to handle or understand this reality and it will result in insanity and a beastly state of existence.

A question we must all ask ourselves is what will happen when man-made technology fails? What will happen when people can no longer get their prescription medications for ADHD, bi-polar disorder, depression, anxiety, paranoia, schizophrenia, etc.? Dis-orders and dis-eases are just what they say; the body is not in order or the body is not at ease. All of these can be cured when we make the revolution within self and learn to breathe the Holy Breath. (Again, my next book will be dedicated to the subject of Spiritual Cultivation of the Holy Breath aka Qigong).

To take all you want Is never good as to stop when you should. Scheme and be sharp And you'll not keep it long. One can never guard His home when it's full of Jade and fine Gold: Wealth, power, pride Bequeath their own doom. When Success and fame come to you, then retire. Dao De Ching.

There are people on this Earth that are striving to maintain control over the masses. These men are Beasts. This is not a conspiracy theory but a fact and common sense when we simply open our eyes (I do not need to point the finger as it is obviously the false "powers" that be and that would be another book).

They do so with so-called laws written on paper and supported by Military Force. They seek to extort the natural resources of the planet and selfishly hoard the "rewards" for the few "elite" who are not elite at all. They only maintain an illusion of control which requires the masses to be dumb, deaf, and blind in order to do so.

They do this through radiation waves from satellites, televisions, radio, microwaves, etc. The masses are kept engulfed in the latest celebrity gossip and scandal as if it is the most important thing in the world. Most eat it up as if it were gospel. This obviously distracts one from focusing on the true reality of self and what is really going on in the world.

Major corporations and conglomerates control and run the media giving you a biased point of view of everything. Movies and music keep us quite distracted with the latest trends. Microwaves radiate food which means you are eating radiation. This breaks down the immune system, lowers your vibration and causes disease. Wars and savagery have run rampant on this planet and it is quite a shame. All we can do is raise our own vibrations and step aside when Mother Earth does what she has to do because the time is now for the Earth to be reborn.

In Governing the World, Let Rule be entrusted to him who treats his rank As if it were his soul; World Sovereignty can be Committed to that man who Loves All People As He Loves himself. Dao De Ching

As Taboos increase, people grow poorer; When weapons abound, the state grows chaotic; As wealth increases, more criminals start. Dao De Ching

Weapons are tools of bad omen.

A multitude slain! And their death is a matter for grief and tears; The victory after a conflict is a theme for a funeral rite. Dao De Ching

Man conforms to the earth; The earth conforms to the sky; The sky conforms to the way; The Way conforms to its own nature. Dao De Ching

Through The Sun and the Shade, Equilibrium comes to the world. Dao De Ching.

Ninety-five percent of men see wombman mostly as a sex object and ninety percent of wombman see men the same way. Innerstand this, the union between man and wombman when dealing with pure love emotion is really one of the closest ways to the Creator (universal creative force that borns all). The union of man's positive masculine polarity penis and wombman's negative feminine (9) in pure love is the true science of creation and perfection.

This indeed is a sacred union as the human bodies are holy temples wherein the spirit and soul lives in this earthly plane. This is the first spiritual ritual on the earthly plane. It is the uniting of two spiritual entities through the human temple vehicles. The penis is the magic wand and the vagina is the cup of life. Furthermore, we must begin to understand Man and Wombman's roles in society/civilization/culture. This is not held sacred nowadays just as the family structure is not held sacred. Most are merely looking for sport sex. The foundation of human life is the family structure which equals The Great Triangle of Life = Man, Wombman, and Child. Of Course, when in Pure Love Union, the sexual ritual would be much more intense, passionate, and enjoyable because of the intense love bond between two spirits being joined as one.

Now for those who cannot see clearly adjust your vision and listen. The earth has a magnetic field of energy around it and this causes polarity which is demonstrated in the North and South poles. One pole having negative polarity and the other having positive polarity. This is a scientific law that maintains the balance of Earth in its rotation and in turn this law governs all life on Earth. This law is also present in the big bang theory and the creation of the universe. The "big bang" is the result of the struggle between dynamic opposites; light and dark, positive and negative. This is the law of creation. This is also referred to as The Great Principle in the Tao/Dao.

The laws of Yin and Yang provide a model of the universe in which we live. Cycles in nature can easily be understood by observing the rhythmic patterns and shifting from one polarity to the opposite. This is not a "mystical" concept. This is very logical. Now we can observe the natural cycles of life.

A man's penis is a positive penetrating force while a wombman's vagina is an absorbing negative nature. Now through the sexual process these dynamic opposites unite in the sexual process exact to the "big bang" and life is created. Furthermore, humans have a magnetic field of energy around us which has been proven scientifically. This magnetic field, of course, has negative and positive polarities. Thus if we are not making the annual revolution within self through the cultivation of our mind, body, and soul through meditation, Qigong, Yoga, Prayer, Chants, or bell tones, our bodies magnetic energy structure will be unbalanced. This is how one increases their vibrational frequency and gets in tune with the higher self/the mind and can better control the physical desires of one's lower self/the body. This is what is referred to as mind over matter and this is what makes humans different from animals.

Most humans were never taught how to cultivate their mind, body, and soul and it is no fault of their own. Now this is where healing can take place based on balancing ones masculine/positive energies with ones feminine/negative energies through the education of cultivation practices. For example, a homosexual male has overt feminine energies that are not being balanced by the natural masculine energies. Balance must be restored when energies are unbalanced. It is the same for a woman who is homosexual, her balance must be restored. Now dealing with the science of creation, balance can be restored through the sexual experience of man/positive and woman/negative uniting together. This is the closest we can get to the universal source/the creator/or simply creation. There simply is no balance in a man on man sexual act or a woman on woman sexual act and nature requires the balance of negative with positive in order for life's cycles to be complete. This cannot be debated.

Furthermore, through the study and practice of Chinese Tonic Herbs, one learns how to use these herbs to balance the Five Elemental energies to restore balance within the human body/temple. The Five Element Theory is used in the practice of Chinese Tonic Herbs to restore energy balance.

The Chinese have been practicing herbalism for several thousand years. That is to say they have much experience in this area. Modern day scientists have studied many Chinese tonic herbs only to confirm that these herbalists were right and exact in their practice. Now, these herbs can be used in combination with cultivation practices as they go hand in hand and complement each other. It is, in fact, encouraged by Chinese herbalist that one practices cultivation through Tai Chi, Qigong, Yoga, meditation, etc., because one must cultivate

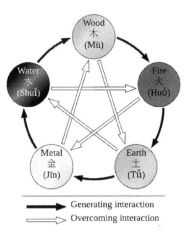

the mind as well as the body to achieve what is referred to as "radiant health." Acupuncture is also combined to restore balance if needed. This is a complete and exact science according to nature. This is "The Way" aka The Tao/Dao.

This is also the reason why homosexuality is not productive to positive progress. When cultivating in a sexual ritual, you need Man and Wombman to maintain harmony and balance according to nature and science. This is the reason there are more nerve endings in the sexual organs and it feels good to procreate for the survival of the human species. Let us stop disrespecting our temples and our universal creator who blessed us with them. Divine Love through education of Spiritual Cultivation practices equals civilization and culture. Man, Wombman, and Child.

Another example of disorder/imbalance is when one is not receiving the proper nutrients and the body becomes deficient. When one's body has a vitamin and or mineral deficiency it can result in mental disorders, such as, depression or anxiety. Reason being is that the body is literally crying out for nutrients. If we don't know this then we think a pill will help. No, the body's chemistry must be balanced with the proper nutrients, vitamins, and minerals. For example, vitamins have multiple benefits to the body so it makes sense that if there is a deficiency then there are multiple effects it has on the body. We need to restore balance. This is simple so let's not make it complicated. *Let thy food be thy medicine.* Hippocrates

Let us look at the spiral. The spiral is expressed in nature everywhere. In Math/Geometry it is found in the Golden Ratio, The Golden Rectangle,

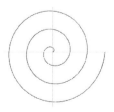

and The Golden Spiral. In 15th century Italy, Leonardo da Vinci saw the balance of perfection of nature represented in the Golden Rectangle. In fact, he drew it into his masterpieces by drawing a

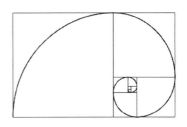

curve through the Golden Rectangle. This showed and proved The Golden Spiral pattern in math and nature.

Pythagoras also loved the spiral as you can see it clearly throughout nature; our DNA spirals, our fingerprints spiral, The Nautilus shell spirals, The Milky Way spirals, whirlpools spiral, tornados spiral, smoke patterns spiral, throw a stone into water and the ripples spiral, etc. You can see energy spirals because of the natural balance and struggle between positive and negative forces, the Supreme Law of Magnetics☺.

A good knot is tied without rope and cannot be loosened.

The Wise Man is always good at helping people, so that none are cast out; he is always good at saving things, so that none are thrown away. This is called applied intelligence.

Surely the good man is the bad man's teacher; and the bad man is the good man's business! If the one does not respect his teacher, or the other doesn't love his business, his error is very great. This is indeed an important secret. Dao De Ching

This means that you have a responsibility to stand up and speak up for what is right and just! We cannot accept just anything from people. Civilization is based upon moral codes and righteous character traits according to the nature of the Way. So when people are going against the Way of nature, it is our responsibility to help them learn the Way of nature so that we may return to nature and evolve into greater Light Beings☺.

K.I.S.S.
Keep It Simple Star
◇◇◇◇◇◇

Human - Hu means spirit and man means flesh.

We are truly spirits who currently live in the flesh. One might ask you, where do you live? The correct answer would be, "I live in my body." The body is the true and living Holy Temple. Life is energy and as energy, it never truly ceases and neither does your spirit. Energy only takes on different forms, potential (dormant) and kinetic (active).

Energy is intelligence. Our physical bodies are our vehicles by which we navigate through our earthly lives interacting, learning, living, loving, growing, and eventually dying. The flesh is weak and can easily be hurt, damaged, and destroyed. That is why it is important to know that our true form is spiritual and is eternal/infinite. We exercise our bodies as we do the mind and we can also exercise and cultivate our spirits by living righteously and focusing on having good intentions in our hearts and minds.

Intentions create karma good or bad. Karma is a dark, murky ether qi (chi) substance that exists as an intelligent entity/entities in another dimension. By having pure heart and mind intentions (which is truly being intelligent) we can resolve all karmic debts from past lives and this life. Energy/ Life vibrates into the ethers of the Universe and makes an imprint like a stone being thrown into water; you can see the ripple effect. This is the same with our thoughts. Our thoughts are born into the ethers and the Universe can feel our intention. Thus the ripple effect will eventually come back to us equally as karma because thoughts are born and alive.

It is not so easy to be "good" all the time as life throws us many obstacles in situations, distractions, tragedies, pain, loss, gain, etc. We experience things such as betrayal, murder, rape, abuse (mental/physical), hate, etc. All of these things make it difficult to maintain our mental health and sanity and quite frankly, life can be crazy. The only thing we can do is to make an honest effort to better understand ourselves and situations. We may do this through knowledge, wisdom, understanding, and, of course, through prayer/meditation.

Let us pray together: *Universal Source, please watch over us all, please walk with us, talk with us, guide and lead us to the path of righteousness, and not the path of destruction, or self destruction. Life can be very confusing given all of the situations we go through, that is why we need your guidance all the time. Please be with us at all times, be conscious in our thoughts and our actions.*

And We Pray: *We pray for food, clothing, and shelter, for the safety, health, and welfare, and for love, peace, and happiness for all humanity. We pray for the healing of the entire Human Family as we pray for the Healing of the Earth.*

The thought is all. Before the body can move, there is thought. In thought, you have negative and positive as in all creation (The Science of a Supernova). It is important to try to see all aspects, both positive and negative, to gain a more clear picture of anything or situation. Thought is energy and energy moves as thoughts do. We can focus our energy/thoughts to accomplish our goals. Thoughts are movements and when thoughts move they create time and space. So thoughts create? But of course, that's why prayer is meditation. We Split Atoms with our thoughts and words are born.

The word God has been studied and analyzed and said to have the most positive vibration over the human body and that, when spoken with love, it can have healing powers. God is Love and Universal Love has the power to heal all. There are healers that are known in the world and all of them have a universal love for all of humanity that is so pure that it is felt simply by their presence in a room. To feel their touch is to be healed of everything that is ailing you. Even some of them are children who have been blessed with this universal love. Others have achieved this through prayer/meditation/fasting/ spiritual practices. This is the Universal Divine Love that the prophet Jesus was said to have healed with.

The word Allah was studied and said to have the second highest vibration with the human body. Again, these are studies and the point is the Universal Love one feels behind the words. In other words, it does not matter the name you call "God-Allah," it is the sincerity and pure intentions behind it that equal positive vibrations of love with genuine healing qualities. As they say, love heals all. So, indeed, it is the feeling behind the words which is the true power. The feeling is the pure thought vibrating the body and even more so through the spoken word.

Let's make a note also that when Man does a study, he first makes a hypothesis which is his/her estimation of what they think will happen. Thoughts create all so the studies of man can be slightly biased. For example, one scientist in China may be studying the same thing as a scientist in London and both scientists will have slightly different outcomes due to their hypotheses. Meaning, their thoughts directly influence the outcome of the study. This has been proven by Quantum Physics.

Now, it is said that we are made in the image of God-Allah (Universal Source), that God-Allah is within us and all life. The Universal Source (God-Allah) is our breath of life, our holy spirit that lives in our body (vehicle) as we first become alive in the body with the first breath. So, God-Allah is within us and that makes us part of God-Allah. However, we are only a droplet of water in the vast ocean of life/light, as it is said. Those who believe themselves to be God-Allah can convince themselves they have no judge and therefore can easily become wicked. That is because of misunderstanding and eating the wrong foods (teachings).

The Universal Source God-Allah does not have to eat or drink to survive. The Universal Source does not have a penis, vagina, anus, nor arms or legs and is not a person. Therefore the Universal Source God-Allah does not have the carnal desires which we possess. We have a desire to eat and drink, and we have a desire to procreate (have sex). We desire material objects, technologies, and things like fame, etc. Do you see the difference? Yes, we can create and have the ability to influence our own cipher of things, only because we are of the Universal

Source, which is energy, which is intelligence, which is again, the thought that creates all. And this indwelling intelligence resides in us all. We will keep it that simple. A lot of times we humans make things difficult when things just boil down to common sense.

The Dao says it the best and to paraphrase, "As soon as you try to give a name to 'God,' you disrespect that which you try to describe." You cannot categorize "God" into one word. In the Tao, they refer to The Un-nameable and the Universal Source. I, personally, consider myself a Taoist/Doaist by nature. The Tao/Dao means "The Way."

One of the most important lessons of the Dao is to learn to blend with nature and live in harmony and peace with one's environment and community. To strive for the betterment of the Self is to strive for the betterment of the all and this is to understand that you are Divine by Nature. This is the Divine Self. In the Tao, it is understood that all are a part of the whole. Yin (negative) and Yang (positive) cannot  exist without each other. That's why the higher lesson is that there is no separation, so it is Yin-Yang. That's why in the Dao Symbol, the Yin is still in the Yang.

There is no mystery God, only The Un-nameable/ Universal Source/Intelligence/Ether/ Energy that creates all and permeates through all, which is all. Let's explore through simple math/numerology/astrology. The Earth is in space as we are, as are all the planets. Ok, so our bodies can be looked at as mini planets. C.M. Bey taught that we are Supreme Moving Planets because we have free will. So while the nine planets have set patterns which they are guided by, we have the power of free will to change our particular orbit (so to speak).

Yes, we definitely can and do get caught up in the same patterns and are creatures of habit, so when we become conscious, we can use our free will to change our patterns or orbit. We can indeed correct old bad habits when our conscious mind is in control of our body. You see, all planets have polarity with magnetic fields around them and we are no different. We have negative and positive polarities ourselves that will pull our planets (bodies) in different directions, right or wrong, good or bad, until we regain Consciousness of the True Self. We may then exercise our free will and navigate our own planet, mind over matter/body.

This definitely takes dedication. The first Law in Dedication is Passion. Passion is the tool one uses to motivate oneself to become dedicated. So, one must first have the passion in order to achieve dedication. Without passion, one just does not have the desire to achieve, so progress and growth are unattainable. With passion, one thinks, feels, and becomes that which is dedication. Art, music, martial arts, sports, meditation, etc., are great examples of this. To become one with your art is the result of one's passion, hard work, and dedication. Hard work equals achievement. When one works hard and achieves, they attain goals that can never be taken away. That is success and a confidence booster. When one has a better view of himself or herself, one has a better view of the world and can thus contribute to the betterment to humanity.

The Way/Dao begot one, And the one, two; And then the two begot three, And three all else. Dao De Ching

Science proves that we are all divine. You see, all life is created from the divine single cell. If you look at the highest magnification of a single cell, encoded is exactly who you are to be from your DNA; from all physical characteristics to even seeing aspects of personality traits. The single cell divides into two, then from two into four, then four into eight, then eight into sixteen, then sixteen into thirty-two, and so on. You form as sacred geometry until the human temple is divinely complete. That means that you are predestined to be who you are going to be from the very start. Indeed, you can conclude that you are part of The Divine Plan as we all are. When you understand this something automatically changes within, one's consciousness becomes activated and one starts to look inward, toward the True Self, for within you resides all the answers.

When one recognizes the True Self, then one takes more responsibility to contribute to humanity as they realize one is the whole. In the Tao, the human body is looked at as a temple and through meditation and alchemy one can strive for longevity and even immortality. Now this concept of immortality is really an achievement of conscious transition through death which is achieved through mastery of the mind, body, and soul through meditation rituals.

A much more basic concept we can strive for on a day to day basis is practicing good health through our diet, exercising, martial arts, qigong (chi gung), and yoga. A healthy body is a healthy mind and practicing good karma is good for one's soul. In other words striving to develop healthy habits for the mind body and doing right by others by committing no crimes against humanity and your environment is to live The Dao/The Way.

Supreme Mathematics Scale 0-9
Applied to Life/Light

◇◇◇◇◇◇

0 = Cipher = 360 degrees

Zero is the universal cosmic womb from which all is created, the darkness of the universe, the potential negative (submissive force). This is can also mean the vagina (notice the similarity), the supreme gate from where all men and women are born on a 90 degree angle.

In life, we will strive to be raised to a perpendicular of 180 degrees, so that we stand straight with the truth. Wombmen are referred to as the Supreme Architect who builds the human body without the sound of hammer or nail in the course of nine months. However, zero represents the universe.

1 = Knowledge

One is the foundation of all things in existence. It is the light of the universe, "out of the darkness came the light," the kinetic positive (action force). This can also mean the penis (notice the similarity), the positive force/thought that sparked from the universal source. Knowledge is everything and that is why every number is only one addition to the next, 2 is just 1+1, and to get to 3, add another 1, and so on.

You can do the knowledge (study) forever, because knowledge is infinite. One is 90 degrees tall which represents man when he is upright and civilized. Knowledge represents the Sun, as the Sun is the foundation of the universe. Elemental Fire and Gold

$$2 = \text{Wisdom}$$

Two is the duality of nature, the dark and the light, the negative and the positive, the yin and the yang, dynamic opposites. Wisdom is wise words spoken because when one can see the duality of a situation, the pros and cons of a situation, then one is wise and will speak wisdom.

Woman is represented as wisdom because of her XX chromosomes, two dominate genes. Wisdom is represented as the Moon and the Moon controls and deals with emotion. A woman's menstrual cycle follows the Moon's cycle of 28 days. The Moon has no light of its own and reflects off of the Sun, these are the true nature of things. Elemental Water and Silver

3 = Understanding

Three is the conclusion/manifestation of knowledge and wisdom, knowledge plus wisdom equal understanding, the best part, the completion. This also represents the Child, the Star, and 360 degrees which equals The Great Triangle of Life; 120 plus 120 plus 120 equal 360. Man, Woman, and Child equal Knowledge, Wisdom, and Understanding. To understand means to have no question and to have no doubt. This is represented by the Child, because the child is the manifestation of the love between man and woman. Fire and Water make Steam. Elemental Air / Ether

4 = Culture Freedom

Culture is your way of life. Once you have understanding, you can start to free the dome (free your mind) of the frustrations of the world by striving to live your culture freely and at peace with nature and with Man, Woman, and Child. This is Culture Freedom, this represents the Earth.

Culture freedom builds a strong foundation 4 x 90 degrees equals 360 degrees square. Also represents the home/ he foundation and customs/culture. Elemental Earth

5 = Power Refinement

Power has many forms; Knowledge is power, physical

power, financial power, even unseen power is in the air we breathe. Power must be refined so not to become out of control or too powerful, in which case, the power will destroy itself. That is false power, so beware.

Five represents the five principles to keep in mind which help to Refine your Power: Love, Truth, Peace, Freedom, and Justice equal the 5 pointed star. Elemental Venus and Saturn

6 = Equality

Equality is to be equal in quality in all of your actions and dealings. This is where Understanding (3) becomes Overstanding by the equation 3 x 2 = (6). Equality is the 6 pointed Star which represents two triangles united, the higher self in control of the lower self (carnal desires). It also means the Great Duality; Positive and Negative as One. Equality is a universal love vibration. Elemental Venus

7 = Geometry = God-Allah's Mathematics

Geometry is the secret to unfolding the Universe, to unfolding the Mind's Eye, and beyond. Seven represents the spirit of God-Allah in Man when the seven chakras (energy centers in body) are cleansed through purity and meditation. This is the true meaning of Godbody; Allah in Man Unified/ Resurrected. This is also represented as the 7 pointed Star.

Elemental Sun and Gold

8 = Build-n-Destroy, Build or Destroy = regeneration

Regeneration is the phoenix rising from the ashes, rebirth, and revitalization. It is also said that you can build and you can destroy all in the same moment. Destroy what you do not need and build on what you do need, be humble in nature and beware of greed. This is a moral, lifelong lesson. Needs and Wants are Different. What you need is what you need to survive, what you want is something extra. Eight is represented in Yin Yang and also in the 8 pointed Star. The question at hand is, "Are you gonna build or are you gonna destroy?" Elemental Saturn and Neptune

9 = Born = to be

Nine is to be born, since there are nine months from conception to birth, nine is represented as the Pregnant Woman, three trimesters, 3 x 3 equaling 9, borns (gives birth to) life cycle 0-9. Again, Woman is the Supreme Architect who builds the temple (body) without the sound of a hammer or nail. Nine is the highest number, after nine you go back to zero and start the cipher again. Nine can only born itself when you multiply it by any number. For example, 9 x 1= 9, 9 x 2=18, 1+ 8 = 9, 9 x 3 = 27, 2+ 7 = 9, 9 x 4 = 36, 3 + 6 = 9, try yourself to go on. And it reborns the number you add to it all the time as well.

For example, 9 + 5 = 14, then add the 1 and the 4 to get 5. Another example: 9 + 6 = 15, 1+ 5 = 6, and so forth! Or, it can be said like this, Born (9) + Power (5) = Knowledge Culture (14) = Power (5), it Borns Power. With the Right Understanding you rename the numbers and Build a higher Overstanding of Supreme Mathematics through application. Nine is obviously represented as the 9 pointed Star.

This will born the Lesson on the Scale 0-9, however, let us review The 12 Jewels as were given by Clarence 13X, The Father, for further innerstanding and building purposes. Twelve values to strive for and twelve steps a man should be able to reach to be civilized. (Again, I am not the founder of this.)

1. Knowledge - to know, to do the knowledge, to study.
2. Wisdom - wise words spoken
3. Understanding - manifestation of knowledge and wisdom
4. Freedom - freeing your mind is true freedom
5. Justice - be just in your actions. One can serve justice or one need not because the universe will balance, be smart, be just
6. Equality - to be equal in quality in all of your dealings
7. Food (Mental and Physical Food) - basic need, let us eat

the right foods so we may digest and get the right nutrients or understanding.

8. Clothing - basic need , provide for oneself and family

9. Shelter - basic need, provide for oneself and family

10. Love - it should be easy to have love in your heart when our basic needs are met

11. Peace - When our needs are taken care of, we should be somewhat at peace

12. Happiness - Highest elevation of understanding

Solar Flares and The Basic Planetary Energy/Color Vibration of the Day

First of all, these are only the basic energies and vibrations of the day. To really study Astrology, there is much more depth to discover as the planets are moving everyday. There are many aspects and angles which the planets form that cause a reaction here on planet Earth. Here, we will only focus on the basic planetary energies and vibrations of the day. We may focus on positive conscious energy daily instead of being totally consumed by the negative of what "could" happen horoscopes. I am for the study of Astrology and Cosmology and have built on the Magnetic Pole Shifts that have been, are, and will continue to happen. However, let us focus on the positive conscious energies of the day because it is known that "Man Makes Rain, Hail, Snow and Earthquakes," but, how? Through our magnetic fields/auras we project our vibration/ emotion (e-motion = energy in motion)/intention into the ethers which has a ripple effect in the universe and on Earth-land just as a stone tossed into water.

Imagine if we could all raise our vibrational frequencies and project world peace. The true revolution would happen at an infinite rate, vibrating at the speed of Light! So, let us align and focus our positive consciousness into the ethers of the Universe and see what goodness we can bring back to our beautiful planet Mother Earth. As stated earlier, we know this is not always easy to do because of our experiences and circumstances which distract and confuse us. However, our purpose on Earth is to grow and evolve to our highest degree so let us look deeper than just surface level. Indeed, life is a series of lessons.

All of our experiences from birth are recorded and locked in our DNA. We never truly forget anything we experience, from our most traumatic to our most happy moment to everything we have smelled, touched and tasted. The DNA does not forget but records this. That is why when people go to counseling or to see a psychiatrist, they always go back to their childhood because therein is the root cause of all issues. Some memories and experiences have been locked away deep into the subconscious and they have to resurface in order for the healing to take place. With that being said, let's look at

Solar Flares and how they have been affecting us.

Solar Flares are explosions that happen on the Sun and they radiate to the Earth. They have a direct effect on the Earth and thus, humans. They particularly affect the human psyche. What they have been doing is actually making these hidden feelings from our traumatic past resurface and if unaware, we have no point of reference as to why we get into these moods or zones.

This explains certain times when you may have felt depressed, angry, frustrated, sad, insane, or whatever. Maybe nothing at all has happened and you don't know why you feel like this. It could be for a few hours, it could be for a day or so, it could be for months at a time, or even for years!

What is happening is that the solar flares are making these experiences resurface and they are released through your DNA. When unaware, we have no reference point and do not understand. The higher our vibration, the better we can deal with this. The lower our vibration, the worse it affects us and can even result in insanity!

This is why the Cultivation Practices are so important. We make the annual revolution within self through the Holy Breath. In addition, all of your ancestors' genes are encoded in your DNA. This explains certain diseases and illnesses that are passed on genetically.

Let us introduce the term Chakra to our vocabulary; one may already be familiar. Chakra is a sanskrit word that literally translates as a "whirling wheel" of energy. Chakras are actually energy centers in the body. Most systems deal with seven chakras, some eight chakras, and the ancients used to deal with fourteen chakras. In a way, chakras can be stimulated and cleansed by merely staring at color vibrations. Other ways to open and cleanse the chakras would, of course, include meditations such as Qigong (Chi-Kung), Energy Work/Breath Control through postures, yoga, Kaballah, etc.

Days of Week

Sunday = Sun Day

The Sun is the foundation of the Universe, it brings all light. Without the Sun there would be no life on Earth. The Sun represents vitality, growth, good health. It can also represent wealth, inner strength, physical strength, exercise, athletics, etc. The Sun deals with your Personality and how the world sees you. Let these be the positive focuses of the day. The Sun rules the Solar Plexus Chakra. The Sun brings the Element Gold to the Earth. Color Vibrations are Gold, Yellow, Orange-Yellow. Wear these colors or, at some point, focus on these colors for the day. Side Jewel: The only real money is Gold and Silver. The Mayans had a very long run in "history" of peace and they had no monetary system. Another Side Jewel: Money is a concept of man, real wealth is within self, do the right things with our money.

Monday = Moon Day

The moon controls the water on the Earth, the tides, a woman's monthly cycle, and brings the element Silver to Earth. The Moon deals with and controls emotions of the central nervous system as the body like the Earth, is three-fourths water. On Mondays let us focus on Understanding our emotions. First we start to do the Knowledge on our emotions within ourselves. Look at our own Negative and Positive E-Motions... feel them...get to know them, so that we may control and better express them. E-motion = Energy in motion.

Water can be calm and still, water can be raging as a wild river or a tidal wave, water can boil and make steam, water can freeze and become cold, one could be easily drowned in water. These are our E-motions and the Water in our bodies.

Water can change fast just like emotions. Every two and a half days, the Moon changes signs. The Moon deals with the Brow/3rd Eye Chakra, dreams and visions. This is sensitivity. Color vibrations are Indigo Blue, Silver, Grey, even light blues, or white. Wear these colors to remind yourself of the positive conscious energy and to calm self. Women can wear white as a symbol of purity as they represent the Moon.

"The moon does not fight. It attacks no one. It does not worry. It does not try to crush others. It keeps to its course, but by its very nature, it gently influences. What other body could pull an entire ocean from shore to shore? The moon is faithful to its nature and its power is never diminished." Deng Ming-Dao, Everyday Tao: Living with Balance and Harmony

Tuesday = Mars Day

Mars brings iron to the Earth and deals with the iron in the body as well. Iron is what nourishes the blood. Mars is known as the Planet of War so it is known to be aggressive in nature. When one has an iron deficiency one can be easily irritable and aggressive in nature. When one has sufficient iron, B12 and other B vitamins, they are calm yet very energetic. On Tuesdays, let us focus on the aggressive force of Mars, using it for inspiration as a positive motivating force. A time for action, getting things done, physical labor, work, great day for exercise (as is any), finishing projects, or whatever motivates you. Channel the warlike energy of Mars only in self-defense and defense of family and loved ones. Mars also deals with the Solar Plexus Chakra. The Color Vibrations are Red and Orange-Red. Wear these colors to accentuate the vibration of consciousness (unless in a neighborhood where it is gang-related and you may become a target. As in everything, use common sense).

Wednesday = Mercury day

Mercury brings Mercury to the Earth. Mercury deals with the Thought, the mind, communication in all forms, speaking, emceeing/rhyming/rapping, singing, writing, song writing, poetry writing, as well as drawing and body language. Mercury also deals with travel, both physical and mental. So Wednesday is a great day to focus on such things.

A day of the mind in mere thought and the thought expressed in so many ways. Remember the Thought is All, and this is one of our Greatest forms of expression and creativity as well as how we communicate. Another example is mental clarity and truth could be the focus of the day, or clear communication could be the focus. It is also a great day for meditation (as is any). Mercury deals with the throat chakra and the Color Vibrations are Turquoise. Greens, blues and yellows which tend to bring similar vibration.

Thursday = Jupiter Day

Jupiter is the largest of the nine planets. It is very gaseous and largely composed of the light elements Hydrogen (H_2) and Helium (He) which Jupiter brings to the earth along with other gases like Ammonia (NH_3), Methane (CH_4), Carbon Monoxide (CO), and more. Jupiter deals with expansion and growth thus making it a good day to focus on such. Give thought to expanding your networks, expanding your business, expanding your mind, expanding your spiritual growth, expanding your horizons; everything from personal growth and development to business growth and development. Jupiter deals with the Navel Chakra and the Color vibrations are Orange, Orange Yellow, and even Browns.

Friday = Venus Day

Venus is known as the planet of beauty, love and art. Venus brings the element of Copper to the Earth. Copper is a great conductor of electricity as is beauty, love and art. All of which can be quite electric and stimulating. Lets us focus on the beauty (inner and outer) of things, on Love (for oneself, for all, and/or personal intimate love between man and woman), and the arts (music and art of all kind). Venus rules the Heart Chakra along with the Sun however, the Color Vibration is Green. All shades.

Saturday = Saturn Day

Saturn rules the home and business. Saturn brings the element Lead to the Earth. Where there is light, Saturn brings darkness. Where there is heat, Saturn brings cold. Where there is joy, Saturn brings sadness. Where there is life, Saturn brings death. Saturn is no joke. When Saturn is involved, it means business. Saturn is also associated with law and justice and is known as Father Time because of its very long seven and a half-year cycle to pass through signs. Saturn day is actually the Seventh Day, the day of rest, the holy Sabbath. So relax, do some house cleaning (literally and figuratively), some yard work, gardening. However, Saturday is still a good day to wrap up some business. Saturn deals with the Root (base) Chakra and the Color Vibration is Black, darkness, and even dark reds. And remember, let us focus on projecting Positive Consciousness/ Intentions into the ethers. The Universe Understands Intention (Projected Will).

Cultivate the Way/Dao yourself, and your Virtue will be genuine. Cultivate it in the home, and its Virtue will overflow. Cultivate it in the village, and the village will endure. Cultivate it in the realm, and the realm will flourish. Cultivate it in the world, and Virtue will be Universal! Dao De Ching

Examples of Application

Ok, let us take past dates and give brief examples on How to "See it." These are quick break downs and could always be expanded, that is why there is space in between.

Supreme Mathematics Scale 0 -9	Vibrations of the Day
1. Knowledge - to know, to do the knowledge, to study.	Sunday = Sun Day
2. Wisdom - wise words spoken	
3. Understanding - manifestation of knowledge and wisdom	Monday = Moon Day
4. Freedom - freeing your mind is true freedom	
5. Justice - be just in your actions. One can serve justice or one need not because the universe will balance, be smart, be just	Tuesday = Mars Day
6. Equality - to be equal in quality in all of your dealings	

7. Food (Mental and Physical Food) -
basic need, let us eat the right foods   so
we may digest and get the right nutrients   Wednesday = Mercury
or understanding.

8. Clothing - basic need , provide for
oneself and family

9. Shelter - basic need, provide for oneself
and family   Thursday = Jupiter Day

10. Love - it should be easy to have love
in your heart when our basic needs are
met

11. Peace - When our needs are taken care
of, we should be somewhat at peace   Friday = Venus Day

12. Happiness - Highest elevation of
understanding   Saturday = Saturn

Let's start with Tuesday, March 30, 2010:

What's tha science for tha day?

Tuesday dealing with Mars, color vibration red, energy aggressive could be negative or positive (be conscious of the energy, use in a motivational way).

Also, tha math of life/light 2day = 3-30-2010.

Understanding (3) + 3 = the equality (6) cipher (0), wisdom (2) cipher (0), knowledge (1) cipher (0), is also = understanding (3).

So, all is being born to born (9) completion which is the daily vibration. The equation is 3+3+0=6, 2+0+1+0=3, 6+3=9

Applying this mathematics into your life is the equation we all have to figure out. Is it so easy that we make it hard? Food for thought...

Ok, let's continue. Wednesday, March 31, 2010:

Whats tha science for tha day?

Wednesday = Mercury = color vibration = turquoise = energy is creative, of the mind, also dealing with communication and travel (physical or mental). "The thought is all. As everything is born of the thought, be conscious of your thoughts."

Also we have the math/life/light of today, 3-31-2010.

Understanding (3) + understanding (3) + knowledge (1) = God-Allah (7) = understanding (3) x 2 = equality (6) + knowledge (1) = God-Allah (7) the knowledge of equality is God-Allah + wisdom (2) + cipher (0) + knowledge (1) + cipher (0) = 3 (understanding).

So, God (7) + understanding (3) = 10 = daily vibration = which is Love in the 12 jewels! The equation is 3+3+1+2+0+1+0= 10.

Let us practice these values in our daily life, true science/

math of life/light.

Ok, I will do one more to bring forth understanding.

Thursday, April 1, 2010:

Today's science is Thursday = Jupiter = Color Vibration Orange = Energy Expansive = Look to expand in positive ways; business, personal, spiritual, mental, musical, etc.

April 1st, is the True and Living New Year according to nature and the zodiac. Everything is born afresh and the spring is the True and Living New Year.

October = 8

November = 9

December = 10

January = 11

February = 12

March 21st is the true New Year, celebrated April 1st in Islam (who are the real April Fools?) and also celebrated by Easter in the Christian world which is the resurrection of the Sun/Chris. It is not Jesus rising from the dead but the Sun rising from the dead of winter. Jesus/Sun of God was born

March 21st. The Earth travels one degree per day around the Sun and on December 25th, it reaches 333 degrees. A Masonic holiday, wouldn't you say? Why do they dull our senses by having us celebrate a new year in the dead of winter when the military and fiscal year starts on April 1, not January 1? This is the true April Fools' Joke. They think you are fools. Time to wake up.

So, getting on with the math of 2day, April 1, 2010.

Culture Freedom (4) + Knowledge (1) = Power Refinement (5) = in Knowledging your culture, you must refine your power so it does not become out of control. Again, the year = Wisdom (2) + Cipher (0) + Knowledge (1) + Cipher (0) = Understanding (3).

So, 4 +1 + 2+ 0 + 1 +0 = Build and/or Destroy (8) Regeneration = Daily Vibration. Again, this is to apply life/ light which all true science and math does.

PAGE FOR YOUR OWN MATH

Symbols:
Tools in the Workshop of the Mind

◇◇◇◇◇◇

From ancient times, all languages were based on numerical vibrations, or values, as well as symbols that taught the basic foundation and understanding of life/light/truth/nature. By providing visual stimulation one can learn on multi-levels☺. This serves a great purpose for civilization and culture as language is one of the very first things we all learn. Now let us break down some symbols and apply them in the Workshop of the Mind.

This represents the Sun, Moon, and Stars, the cosmic universe from which life stems. This also represents life on Earth as we are governed by the Cosmic Laws of the Universe. So, in turn, this also represents

Man (120degrees), Wombman (120degrees), and Child (120degrees) to equal 360 degrees of life. This is also referred to as the Great Triangle of Life; The Human Family.

The All Seeing Eye of Horus represents one's 3rd Eye when opened (the pineal gland). This also represents the Higher Self or the I Self. The pyramid represents the human body or

lower self in which we must build a strong moral foundation to master. When the capstone is shown connected to the pyramid, it represents that the Higher Self is in control of the Lower Self.

However, on the one dollar Federal Reserve Debt instrument, the pyramid with the capstone not connected. This has a dual meaning. First, the All Seeing Eye for them represents the "illuminati," the ones who are controlling and

conquering the masses. The pyramid represents the humans they turned into Corporations via Admiral Maritime Laws via

Birth Certificates, Social Security Cards, Marriage Licenses, Drivers Licenses, etc. Civil Law is the Law of the Land and Admiral Maritime Law is the Law of Commerce and Trade on the open seas. So, the pyramid with the capstone disconnected also represents the masses of people who are dumb, deaf, and blind to this. In other words, those who are not in control of their Higher Selves but are instead ruled by their Lower Selves. Each brick represents a corporation aka human being.

In the Workshop of the Mind, Geometry can be applied. G stands for Geometry and also for God. The letter G corresponds with the number 7, hence G7. The compass is used to circle one's owns cipher and keep it within the bounds of Righteousness. The Square is used so that we do not cut any corners and we square our actions making them Right and Just like right angles, 90 degrees precise.

This was first referred to as the Hexalpha. This symbol represents the principle, "As above, so below," meaning Man/Wombman is a microcosm of the macrocosm (Universe). We are a smaller version or model of the Universe. Also, the top triangle is an ancient symbol that used to represent Air or the Mind. The bottom triangle used to represent Earth or the Body. So again, this is another symbol representing Mind over Matter, or the Higher Self over the Lower Self. Through Cultivation, this represents regeneration of the human temple; the phoenix rising from the ashes.

Mathematically we can break this down as well.

Triangle 1 = 120 degrees, 120 degrees, 120 degrees = 360 degrees of Higher Self

Triangle 2 = 120 degrees, 120 degrees, 120 degrees = 360 degrees of Lower Self

Together, they equal 720 degrees of mastery within Self.

Also, 1+2 = 3. So, 3+3+3 = 9 = born = the cycle of life's creation, 0-9 months from conception to birth.

Also, 360 = 3+6 = 9. And, 720 = 7+2 = 9.

One could also see the 3+3+3 as the 33 3rd Degrees in masonry or the 33 3rd vertebrae in the spinal column. When one uses the Strong Grip of the Lions Paw or the Solar Energy of Crown Chakra = Positive Polarity to pull the Kundalini/Qi/ Lifeforce from the base of the spine or the Negative Polarity where it is buried in a shallow grave. This moves it up the spinal column to energize the Mind/Pituitary and Pineal Gland. This is done in every Spiritual Cultivation system.

I will keep this very simple. The Universal Cross is a representation of the Zodiac, the 12 constellations that govern our Solar System. The Cross points to the Cardinal Signs of the Zodiac representing the  seasons and showing that the True and Living New Year is spring, when the Life Cycle renews itself. How can one have a new year in the dead of winter?

This is the Universal Cross that the Only Begotten Sun of the Universe was upon and sacrificed his Life for Humanity. Get it? Jesus being a representation of the Sun in  which the 12 constellations/12 disciples cipher around.

I leave you with these symbols which have been used for ages to show the Science of The Universe and Nature.

In paraphrasing C.M. Bey, "It only takes a short book to reveal the truth, yet it takes a long book to hide history and science."

More Food for Thought and

Some References☺

Chinese Tonic Herbs, by Ron Teegaurden

Clocks of Destiny, Books 1 and 2, C.M. Bey

Circle 7 Koran

Dao De Ching

Dhammapadra

Supreme Mathematics as taught by

Clarence 13, The Father

Simply Study Numerology☺

Simply Study Astrology☺

The Dancing Wu Li Masters, Gary Zukav

The Dao of
Math and Science
Ireality El

25997491R00047

Printed in Great Britain
by Amazon